SnoCross

Connie Colwell Miller
AR B.L.: 2.8
Points: 0.5   MG

X GAMES

SnoCross

by Connie Colwell Miller

Content Consultant:
Ben Hobson
Content Coordinator
Extreme Sports Channel
United Kingdom

Reading Consultant:
Barbara J. Fox
Reading Specialist
North Carolina State University

Capstone press

Mankato, Minnesota

Blazers is published by Capstone Press,
151 Good Counsel Drive, P.O. Box 669, Mankato, Minnesota 56002.
www.capstonepress.com

Library of Congress Cataloging-in-Publication Data
Miller, Connie Colwell, 1976–
   SnoCross / by Connie Colwell Miller.
   p. cm. — (Blazers. X games)
   Summary: "Describes the X Games SnoCross event, including the course,
how the event is done, and star riders" — Provided by publisher.
   Includes bibliographical references and index.
   ISBN-13: 978-1-4296-1292-0 (hardcover)
   ISBN-10: 1-4296-1292-4 (hardcover)
   1. SnoCross Championship Racing (Game) I. Title. II. Series.
GV1469.35.S6M55 2008
794.8 — dc22   2007032827

Essential content terms are bold and are defined at the bottom of the page where they first appear.

Editorial Credits
Carrie A. Braulick and Abby Czeskleba, editors; Bobbi J. Wyss, set designer;
   Alison Thiele, book designer; Jo Miller, photo researcher

Photo Credits
AP Images/Jack Dempsey, cover; Nathan Bilow, 20–21
Corbis/Duomo, 28–29
Getty Images Inc./Brian Bahr, 11, 17; Doug Pensinger, 5, 18–19;
   Jamie Squire, 12; WireImage/Allen Kee, 23; Mike Ehrmann, 14, 24, 26–27;
Riccardo S. Savi, 6, 7; Scott Clark, 8

1 2 3 4 5 6 13 12 11 10 09 08

Table of Contents

A Sudden Comeback

SnoCross riders revved
their engines. It was the start
of the 2006 X Games SnoCross
event. This was an important
race for Blair Morgan.

Morgan trailed the top three
riders at the beginning of the race.
Morgan's chances of winning didn't
look good. The leader, Levi LaVallee,
had a nine-second lead over Morgan.

Blair Morgan

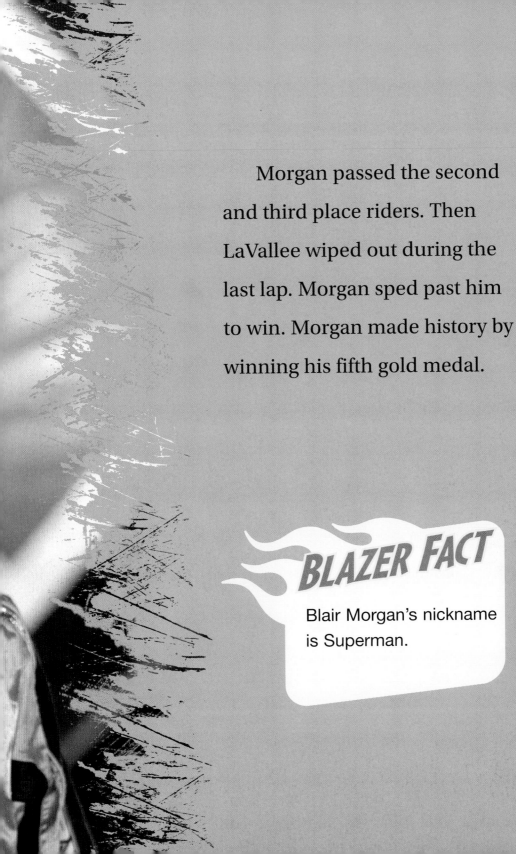

Morgan passed the second and third place riders. Then LaVallee wiped out during the last lap. Morgan sped past him to win. Morgan made history by winning his fifth gold medal.

BLAZER FACT

Blair Morgan's nickname is Superman.

Berms, Turns, and Bumps

SnoCross riders whip their snowmobiles around a short, snowy course. The first rider to speed across the finish line takes home the gold medal.

BLAZER FACT

People who spend a lot of time snowmobiling are called "sledheads."

SnoCross gets its name from the sport of **motocross**. SnoCross courses include sharp turns, jumps, and bumps just like motocross courses.

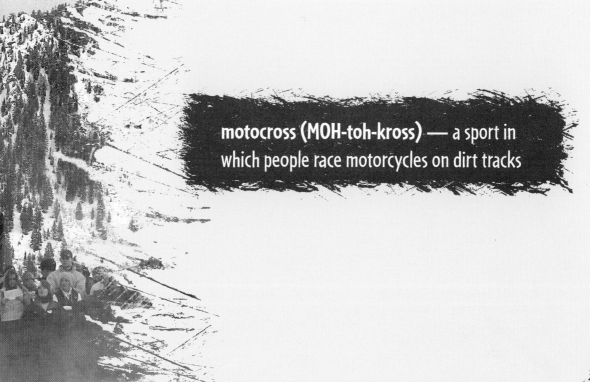

motocross (MOH-toh-kross) — a sport in which people race motorcycles on dirt tracks

A SnoCross race isn't just about speed. Riders need skill and focus. They lean sharply around **berms** and get bumped by other riders.

berm (BURM) — a banked turn or corner on a SnoCross course

Getting the Gold

SnoCross riders race in **heats** at the X Games. The top 12 riders from the heats compete in the final competition. The final competition is 15 laps long.

heat (HEET) — a round in a competition; the top finishers from a heat race move on to the final event.

The winner gets a gold medal along with thousands of dollars. Medals and smaller cash prizes are also awarded for second and third place.

SnoCross Course Diagram

track official

jump

finish line

rhythm section

21

SnoCross Legends

Only the best SnoCross riders are invited to compete in the X Games. Blair Morgan is one of the all-time greats.

Tucker Hibbert

Other talented riders are
Steve Martin, Levi LaVallee,
and Tucker Hibbert. In 2000,
Hibbert became the youngest
rider to win a gold medal.

Tucker Hibbert was
15 years old when he
won his first gold medal.

Blair Morgan

Even the top riders work hard to improve their skills. Practicing helps riders become faster. The faster they ride, the more exciting SnoCross is for their fans.

Tucker Hibbert

Race to the Finish!

Glossary

berm (BURM) — a banked turn or corner on a SnoCross course

competition (kahm-puh-TI-shuhn) — a contest between two or more people

course (KORSS) — a set path; SnoCross riders compete on a course.

heat (HEET) — a round in a competition; the top riders from a heat go on to the final event.

motocross (MOH-toh-kross) — a sport in which people race motorcycles on dirt tracks

rev (REV) — to make an engine run quickly and noisily

Read More

Doeden, Matt. *Snowmobiles.* Horsepower. Mankato, Minn.: Capstone Press, 2005.

Maurer, Tracy Nelson. *Snocross.* Radsports Guides. Vero Beach, Fla.: Rourke, 2003.

McClellan, Ray. *Snocross.* Torque: Action Sports. Minneapolis: Bellwether Media, 2008.

Internet Sites

FactHound offers a safe, fun way to find Internet sites related to this book. All of the sites on FactHound have been researched by our staff.

Here's how:
1. Visit *www.facthound.com*
2. Choose your grade level.
3. Type in this book ID **1429612924** for age-appropriate sites. You may also browse subjects by clicking on letters, or by clicking on pictures and words.
4. Click on the **Fetch It** button.

FactHound will fetch the best sites for you!

Index